CAN DO

Serious Fun: Games for 10-14 year olds

Books in the series:

 Familiar Things
by Sally Thomas

 Eco–Ventures
by Hannah Sugar, Kids' Clubs Network

 Serious Fun: Games for 4–9s
by Phill Burton, Dynamix

 Whatever the Weather
by Jane Gallagher

 Cool Creations
by Mary Allanson, Kids' Clubs Network

 Serious Fun: Games for 10–14s
by Phill Burton, Dynamix

 Sticks and Stones
by Sharon Crockett

Series Foreword

Children and young people of all ages should be able to initiate and develop their own play. Adult involvement should be based on careful observation, appropriate consultation and response to what the children need in terms of their development at this time and in this place.

Play is freely chosen personally directed behaviour motivated from within. Adults can create the best possible conditions for play: the time, space, materials, safety and support for children to develop the skills and understanding they need to extend the possibilities of their play. The degree to which the children and young people are able to make any activity their own will determine its success as a play opportunity rather than simply 'entertainment', a means of 'keeping them busy' or producing 'something to take home to parents'.

Many of the ideas in these books are not new. Indeed play games and creative activities are passed on across many generations and between different cultures across the world, constantly being adapted and changed to suit a new time, a new group of children, a new environment.

We have acknowledged sources and sought permission wherever it has been possible to do so. We hope, and indeed anticipate, that the ideas in these books will be adapted and developed further by those that use them and would be very interested to hear your comments, thoughts, ideas and suggestions.
www.thomsonlearning.co.uk/childcare

Annie Davy

CAN DO
Serious Fun: Games for 10-14 year olds

By **Dynamix**
Series Editor: **Annie Davy**

THOMSON

Australia • Canada • Mexico • Singapore • Spain • United Kingdom • United States

THOMSON

Games for 10–14 year Olds

Copyright © Dynamix 2002

The Thomson logo is a registered trademark used herein under licence.

For more information, contact Thomson, High Holborn House, 50–51 Bedford Row, London, WC1R 4LR or visit us on the World Wide Web at: http://www.thomsonlearning.co.uk

British Library Cataloguing-in-Publication Data
A catalogue record for this book is available from the British Library

ISBN 1-86152-839-6

First edition 2002

Typeset by Bottle & Co., Banbury, UK

Illustrations by Les Evans

Printed in Croatia by Zrinski

Text design by Bottle & Co.

Contents

Introduction and Information Gathering Games

Trust and Team Games

Letting Off Steam Games

Parachute Games

Small Space and Small Group Games

End, Celebration and Wind Down Games

Series Introduction

The CAN DO series is an intensely practical resource for children who attend childcare settings, drop in centres or playsettings out of school, and for those of you who work with them in these settings. Anyone working with children, whether as a trainee, an experienced manager or as a volunteer will sometimes get tired, feel jaded or simply seek new inspiration. Whether you are a childminder, a playworker, a family centre worker or a day nursery assistant or manager, you will find a rich source of ideas for children of all ages in the CAN DO series. In these books you will find practical answers to the difficult 'CAN DO' questions which are often asked of adults working with children:

- Child coming in from school, 'What can I do today?'
- Parent visiting a childminder: 'What exactly can the children do here?'
- Playworker or Childcare worker at a team meeting: 'What can we do to extend the range of play provision here?'

The series is structured towards 3 different age ranges— 0–3, 4–9 and 10–14, but many of the books will be used successfully by or with older or younger children. The books are written by authors with a wide range of experience in working with children and young people, and who have a thorough understanding of the value of play and the possibilities and constraints of work in childcare and play settings.

Each activity is introduced with a 'why we like it' section, which explains why children and adults who work with children have found this to be something that they enjoyed, or that has enhanced their play provision. Many of the activities also have 'Snapshots' and 'Spotlight' boxes which expand on the possibilities as developed by children, or an approach you can take in working with children. These sections are intended to help you reflect on your work and the quality of what is provided.

The ideas in this series are intended to be playful, inclusive and affordable. They are not based on any prescribed curriculum, but they could be used to enrich and develop almost any setting in which children play and learn. They do not rely on expensive toys and equipment; they are environmentally friendly and are peppered with practical tips and health and safety checkpoints.

Language used in the book

YOU (the reader): The books are addressed to children and the adults who work with them together. Older children will be able to use the books themselves or with a little co-operation from adults. There are some activities where adult supervision or assistance will be required (in developing and supervising safe working with tools for example) and this is highlighted where relevant.

SETTING: We have used the term 'setting' rather than club, scheme, centre, etc. as the generic term to describe the range of contexts for childcare and playwork including childminders' homes. The 'Snapshot' draw on a range of different settings to illustrate the development of some of the activities in practice.

PLAYLEADER: This term is predominantly used in the 4–9 and 10–14 series, as this is the most familiar generic term that covers adults working with these age groups in out of school settings.

Games for 10–14 year olds

This book gives ideas for games, which, in our experience, work with young people in a wide range of settings. We have tried them all and had a serious amount of fun playing them and teaching them, but young people aged 10–14 are more ready to challenge a leader than younger children so not all these games will work for everyone.

Introduction

Have a look at the world's worst games leader to work out what you can avoid.

Here are a few tips to running a successful games session.

TRY THE GAMES FIRST with a group you know well. Put new games in with familiar ones or work with a friendly supporter to help remind you if you miss out a bit—particularly the safety messages. You may want to write a list of memory joggers on a piece of paper, or have a big list on the wall.

USE THE EXPERTS. Young people are likely to have great ideas and if you take their ideas on, the game will be owned by the group. They will also help you to adapt the games.

CHOOSE YOUR GAMES ACCORDING TO THE NEEDS OF YOUR GROUP. Are they in need of focussing? Are they about to explode with energy? Do you want to play one game for twenty minutes or lots of different games for a few minutes each?

BE READY TO SUPPORT ANYONE JOINING IN—keep your play inclusive for all potential players

COMMUNICATE CLEARLY. Be honest, you don't have to shout or patronise your group to get your message across.

KEEP YOUR COOL if you get wound up by the young people, realise that the game you were playing hasn't held their interest enough and that they have started playing a new game called, 'Wind up the grown up'. The rules of this game are that they try to find a psychological chink in your protective amour and apply a bit of pressure —and they do that until you behave irrationally! Then they sit back and enjoy the entertainment. If and when you realise this is happening try to get them to choose a game that you will all enjoy rather than one which makes everyone feel bad.

KEEP IT EMOTIONALLY AND PHYSICALLY SAFE but that doesn't have to mean boring—there is a line between challenging and dangerous and you need to recognise that for all players.

STAY FLEXIBLE AND USE YOUR IMAGINATION. Be ready to change your games programme and your games.

BE PREPARED TO BE A BIT ENERGETIC, though if you aren't feeling energetic play some calming games then some energy builders.

THINK ABOUT WHAT WORKED AND WHAT DIDN'T. At the end of the session, you will need to check on how others felt it went, how much did they enjoy? Use this information to plan what comes next.

HAVE FUN and don't worry about doing the games right—a mess up could result in a whole new game.

Introduction and Information Gathering Games

Spotlight

If you are working with a new group, you need to find out about them and they need to find out about you and each other. You want to set the tone and boundaries and give them a good feeling about being part of the group. They may know each other well (you need to know that) or they may be in groups who do know each other but with a few isolated or new members. Playing warm-up games to get the young people to share and swap information in a fun and not too threatening way will make playing with them a lot easier as it will be their games session too.

Introduce Your Clothes

Why we like it

It is a straightforward, introductory one-to-one exercise

You can make your answers as personal and revealing as you want to.

You are not asking about people's skills or hobbies or dreams or ideas and there is usually something to say, a story to tell or an opinion about clothes, even if it is 'I hate these socks because...'

Some of the stories may be funny, some moving, some very revealing and the boring stories are often short

We have never had any safety or disclosure problems

It's a good way of getting over the first-introductions barrier

It is a game that can work even if participants have speech or language impairment. It can be adopted easily.

How many can do it

Any number.

Where you can do it

Anywhere that people can talk in pairs safely and without too many interruptions.

What you might need

Can use pens and paper to help remember.

Safety Check

Information may be shared with the group so tell everyone at the start that they need to be happy to share what they tell with everyone.

How you can do it

1. Get into pairs (encourage mixing so no-one is with a close friend) and give simple, clear instructions, for example, 'Find out your partner's name and introduce one item of clothing or jewellery you are wearing. Listen to each other and then introduce your new partner to the whole group trying to remember and recount the story you have just heard.'

2. The person introducing the game can give an example of a simple or deeper story through their clothes. 'These are my trainers. I got them half price in a local sale' or 'This is my ring. My partner got it from her father and it has the family name engraved inside it and losing it would bring the family curse down on my head.'

Snapshot

A player who had recently arrived from Africa introduced his shoes with this story: 'They are my first pair of new shoes, my village bought them for me when they knew I was coming to this country'.

The group had been told so much more in that moment than we expected and the game became much more valuable.

Similarities and Differences

Why we like it

It can be played anywhere

It can be played not only with any age group but with real mixes of age

It is good for helping people to realise that they can usually find something in common with others.

How many can do it

2–8

Where you can do it

Anywhere!

Spotlight

This game was used in a Swansea Comprehensive group when training pupils to be peer mentors. It is often used in anti-bullying and team-building sessions as a way of showing how many similarities people share irrespective of behaviour.

How you can do it

1. Sit in a small circle. The first part of the game is for the group to find things you have in common, for example, you have to talk to each other and find out one food that you all like. If one person in the group doesn't agree with the food, then he or she has to find another. Other examples of questions are:

One drink that you all really like

A type of music that you all like

A TV programme that you all like

2. You can make up your own questions. You could ask the questions separately or you could create a scenario, such as, 'Imagine that you are locked in a room for a day. You are allowed to choose one meal, one kind of drink and you can choose one TV programme. Everybody in your group must be happy with the things chosen.'

3. Once you have agreed similarities, you can discover differences, such as, 'Each person in the group must think of one thing that they have tried eating that nobody else in the group has.' Or 'Each person must come up with one film they've seen that nobody else has.' Remember to get the feedback because this can be quite amusing—worms, paint and woodlouse poo have been examples of strange food!

4. The outcome of this game, and the main thing to point out to the group, is usually that it is much easier to find things in common with other people than it is to find differences.

Country Greetings

Why we like it

It's fun and a bit chaotic

It promotes understanding of cultural differences

Physical contact.

How many can do it

9 or more.

Where you can do it

Somewhere with enough space to 'mingle'.

Spotlight—Celebrating Differences

Games such as this can be a good way of sharing the richness of cultural diversity. Be sure that it is done in a way that allows players to respect and enjoy the range of people they are with as well as getting more information about cultures that they have never experienced.

Games can also get players to recognise that they share similarities with the people whom they least expect to have things in common with. You might uncover surprising similarities. For example, try using people's music collections in Similarities and Differences and you will find that bizarre and embarrassing records will be shared by the most unexpected people!

How you can do it

1. Divide into groups of 3–8 people, making at least 3 groups. Each group is a country with its own way of saying 'hello'. If you are introducing the game, explain that everyone will have 2 minutes to visit and learn from as many other countries as possible. You may need to visit each country to demonstrate the actions of different countries, for example:

France—kiss both cheeks and say Bonjour

Mongolia—clasp elbows and shake

India—hold hands together, bow and say namaste

Inuit—rub noses

Maori—touch foreheads (be careful of headbutting!)

Malaysia—clasp hands and bow

Japan—hold hands by side and bow

Zimbabwe—Shake left hands, stamp and say 'Jambo'

Add your own!

2. When all groups have practiced their 'hellos', repeat the instructions to visit and learn and then say 'GO'.

3. After a couple of minutes, stop and ask people to return to groups.

4. Ask each group who they met, where they were from, and how they say 'hello'.

Snapshot

With one group that had a good mix of cultural backgrounds, we asked for further cultural greetings. This provided an opportunity to learn more about and celebrate each other's origins and lead to discussions about cultural differences, acceptance and anti-racism.

With another drama group we created a dramatic outer space scenario and invented new greetings that the aliens might use.

Do You Want New Neighbours?

Why we like it

It's a good warm up game

It's a useful name game

It's a physical running around game

Even when it's sabotaged, it works to learn names.

How many can do it

10 or more.

Where you can do it

A space with enough room for a circle of sitting or standing players.

Snapshot

One group who knew each other's names really well played this game using their middle names (those who didn't have middle names chose exciting and exotic new names) and the game worked really well as an icebreaker.

How you can do it

1. Get into a circle and ask everyone to check that they know the names of the 2 players standing next to them.

2. Approach one player and ask question 1: Do you want new neighbours? The player can answer 'Yes, I want new neighbours' or 'No'. If she answers 'No', ask her to name his present 2 neighbours so the group can hear. If she answers fast enough, you move on. If not, she must take your place.
If she answers 'Yes I want new neighbours', then ask question 2: Who do you want? She can answer either
a) Anybody or
b) Name 2 other players in the circle
If she says 'a' then everyone in the circle has to change places and you can try to find an empty space, leaving the last player to find a place to continue the game and ask the questions. If she says 'b' then her present neighbours and the newly chosen neighbours must try to change places before you get into the spare space before them. Again the last person to get back into the circle is the one who continues to game, and asks the questions.

3. The game gets better as a name game if a few people say 'anybody' as the circle gets muddled around.

Trust and Team Games

Spotlight

Building up physical trust in a group can underline the idea that you are not the only person who is responsible for keeping it safe—every player has to keep it safe for everyone else. Keeping a group of 10–14 year olds safe has to be mutually agreed as you can only point out the dangers you know about. You cannot police safe behaviour at all times or be everywhere at once. However good a safety head you have, if someone really wants to do something risky, they will do it just as you turn away!

Team games can build up team spirit but beware of teams getting too fixed. This can lead to your players 'putting down' other teams. Having said that, team games are really popular and the competition between teams, if it is light and fun, can be a strong element of a games session.

Points of Contact

Why we like it

It's a very good team builder

It involves problem solving

It also involves plenty of physical contact

People get into difficult or silly positions.

How many can do it

4+

Where you can do it

Space where people can stand and move around a little.

Snapshot

We played this game with a group of senior youth club workers with one person in each team being chosen as a 'director' who tried to get the group to 'get it right' as quickly as possible. Everyone had a go and the differences between groups was noted. It worked well as an introduction to discussing leadership.

In a British juggling festival a version of this game involved creating a juggling monster which had to have as few points of contact with the ground as possible and the greatest number of objects juggled in the air. The resulting human pyramid with balls and clubs firing into the air was used in a very entertaining competition (points were awarded for skill, number of objects and, most of all, style and imagination!).

How you can do it

1. Get into teams of equal size and explain that each team currently has twice the number of 'points of contact' with the ground as there are members of the group (for example, teams of 6 people have 12 points of contact, assuming that you are all standing on 2 legs).

2. Set different challenges of numbers using points of contact with the floor, for example, with 8 points of contact, 4 of the group of 6 people (see above) would have to stand on 1 leg, the remaining 2 could remain on 2 legs.

3. Make more specific demands, for example, at least 1 hand and a forehead. This makes the whole process more complicated (and more fun). Using fingers, knees, toes, etc. the number of points can be increased enormously.

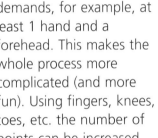

Safety Check

The game may involve some lifting, piggybacks, etc.

Shape Challenge

Why we like it

It is a good group bonding exercise

The challenges get more daring, so 2 or more rounds are worth playing

It needs imagination and gets people trying out simple (or quite complex) group acrobatics.

How many can do it

At least 3 per team.

Where you can do it

A large space where people can make human sculptures.

What you might need

Nothing (furniture may be used).

Safety Check

Make sure the team members look after each other. You could use gym mats or other safe landing surface. Beware, human pyramids can be very unstable.

How you can do it

1. Divide into teams of roughly equal size. Challenge each group to form a single geometric shape or letter by joining their bodies together. The shapes are admired one at a time by the other groups. Then ask each group to come up with a shape or object for the another group to make.

2. The first challenge can be simple but try to persuade the groups to set more difficult and imaginative challenges for the next group around to complete.

3. Limit the time for completing the shape according to the time you have for the game and how experienced the group are at teamwork.

Examples of shapes we have seen made are waterfalls, Blackpool Tower with a lift, an elephant riding a bicycle, and a complete bathroom suite with flushing toilet.

4. There is no limit to the potential for challenge in this game and the more interesting the shapes involved, the more fun for the participants.

Snapshot

An environmental playscheme added a new dimension by using a parachute and sending groups underneath to create rainforest scenes and so on. The rest of the group would then count down and 'mushroom' the parachute to reveal the scene ('mushrooming' is described in more detail in the Parachute Games section).

Vampires

Why we like it

It is a calming trust-based game

It can be quite dramatic

It allows people to scream if they want to

It will go on and on as there will never be a point when all the people are 'vampires' or 'victims'.

How many can do it

More than 10 and at least 4 safety monitors.

Where you can do it

A large empty space that is cleared of any dangerous obstructions.

What you might need

Avoid using blindfolds unless you have the trust of the group and/or the agreement of the group.

Spotlight—Using Drama

Making games dramatic can give them a new lease of life. Telling wild stories about a game can make it more memorable and you can start to make your games relevant to themes and the interests of the group. Linking between a games session and a drama session could get your group warmed up both physically and imaginatively without being too stressful!

How you can do it

1. Choose a person to be a 'vampire'. The vampire walks around looking for new 'blood' to become vampires as well. The vampire keeps her eyes closed and walks around slowly with her arms extended. The rest of the group also have their eyes closed.

2. The aim of the vampire is to grasp the shoulders of an innocent victim who must let out a piercing scream before becoming another vampire. Vampires will only be turned back into 'innocents' if they are grabbed by another unsuspecting vampire. They should let out a large sigh of relief and continue to walk about as a potential victim.

3. The first vampire must be chosen carefully to make sure she will not sabotage the game by a) not hunting new victims or b) moving around with her eyes open.

Safety Check

As the group will have their eyes closed, the safety monitors must protect them from the sharp ends of the room. They can also keep an eye out for people keeping their eyes open!

phew!

Snapshot

For a Halloween party, we improved the drama with more story and the introduction of other characters such as 'werewolves' who had to howl as they caught a victim and 'witches' who cackled as they caught new bodies. We used a range of noises plus some simple costumes and props (peeled grapes are particularly horrible!).

Pass the Picture

Why we like it

Quiet co-operation

It stresses teamwork

Its good for communication.

How many can do it

6 or more.

Where you can do it

Anywhere.

What you might need

Paper and pens, a simple line drawing.

Snapshot

On a team-building day with a school in the South Wales Valleys, once they had passed on their information, players were drawn to one side and asked to generate a list of 'top tips for communication'. They were asked to think about those things that would have made the game easier, such as giving clear descriptions. The picture drawn involved local landmarks to make it relevant to the group but also information that was easily distorted.

One player had 'cheated' when, as the front person, she hopped to the back to help the artist. This was drawn out as a 'top tip for communication' as it cut out the middle men!

How you can do it

1.   The game is a visual version of Chinese Whispers. Before starting, have a picture prepared. Create equal teams of 4–10 people.

2.   Organise yourselves with each team having a person with a good memory (the 'rememberer') at the front and a good artist at the back. Allow the rememberer to look at the original picture for 1 minute, then pass a verbal description down the line in Chinese Whisper style until last person tries to recreate the picture.

3.   Once you've passed on your info, you must be quiet.

4.   When complete, the artists come up to front and compare to original.

Safety Check

Have a rule about non-offensive pictures.

Sculpting

Why we like it

It's a good physical trust game that does not involve falling or bashing into objects

It allows people to choose their role and level of participation

It makes people laugh and think.

How many can do it

Groups of 3. Minimum number of groups,1.

Where you can do it

Any safe space.

Spotlight

You can use the game to explore emotions, to work on details like hand and feet position or the expression on the face. You could also suggest sculpting hands if the full body contact is difficult or not appropriate for the group. You could try this game with the players who are 'clay' keeping their eyes closed too. This stops them from being too helpful to the sculptor because they may have seen what the end result should look like.

How you can do it

Get into threes, and each group must choose a 'sculptor', a 'model' and 'lump of clay'.

1. Each sculptor must close his eyes after he knows where the model and clay are standing.

Model   clay   Sculptor

2. The clay should crouch down and become a flexible, moveable blob that will stay in the position that it is placed by the sculptor.

3. The model should get into a position with his body that he can stay in for a few minutes.

4. The sculptor, with his eyes still closed, must then go and feel the shape that the model has chosen (you can tell everyone that there is no need to feel every bit of the body as there are some parts which the model cannot change!).

Safety Check

This game involves touching and being touched. You may need to point out, as carefully as you can, the concept of safe touching and that unsafe touching is not OK.

5. The sculptor must remember the shape of the model and move the clay into a copy of the shape.

6. When the sculptor is satisfied with his work (it's as good a likeness as he can get) he opens their eyes and the 3 people should suggest how he could have made it better (details they missed and so on).

Pass the Buck

Why we like it

It is a trust game—you are passing control of the game over!

It is a chance for a lot of imaginative and challenging play

It can lead to very valuable discussions about the use and abuse of power

The game is a good lead into creating rules or ways of making it work as the things you learn from unfair use of power can then allow people to discuss rights and responsibilities.

How many can do it

More than 5.

Where you can do it

Anywhere.

Snapshot

In one group of young men, the session became an increasingly tough work-out where each person who had the buck invented more and more extreme physical exercises to get everyone worn out. It could have got really difficult (for the people running the game!) but a few well inserted grunts and a bit of humour about the army (!) prevented the game getting too vicious.

How you can do it

1. Choose an object (it can be a shoe, hat, conch shell, etc.) and explain that having this object means you are completely in charge of everyone in the room.

2. Whoever has the object must give instructions to everyone else and they are to obey those instructions without a murmur! Make the instructions possible for everyone to fulfill and not too humiliating or bossy.

3. If you use your power fairly, the people you pass the buck to may not be vindictive or too outrageous either. You also inform everyone that they have a right to shout 'Stop' if the instructions are unsafe or unfair (you can limit the number of vetoes to 1 or 2 per person).

4. The idea is to only keep 'the buck' for a short time and then to pass it to someone else.

Spotlight

Here are some examples of instructions we have used during this game:

Everyone behave like they are frozen

You all have to make the sound of a space alien

No-one smile

Everyone turn into a professional footballer or disco dancer

All breathe very very slowly

Safety Check

There may need to be a stop or veto clause to overrule any unsafe instructions.

Nightclubbing

Why we like it

It looks a bit like musical chairs, the party game, but does not involve people being 'out'.

It becomes a greater physical contact game as the rounds go on.

What you might need

Old newspaper or large hula hoops or mats of some sort (about 6 or more of 1 of the above pieces of equipment are needed)

A source of music such as a cassette player or CD player would add to the game.

How many can do it

More than 10.

Where you can do it

A reasonable amount of empty space with room to dance for all the players.

How you can do it

1. Lay the 'night clubs' on the floor (double page spreads of newspaper, hoops or mats and explain that they are the local night clubs. The players are told that, in the game, there are 2 times of the week: the time of gloom and the time in the nightclub!

2. During the time of gloom the players have to wander around not treading on the clubs and then when you call out 'Saturday night' everybody has to get into a club and dance about to the music. Everyone must have at least 1 foot inside.

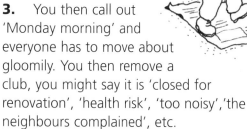

3. You then call out 'Monday morning' and everyone has to move about gloomily. You then remove a club, you might say it is 'closed for renovation', 'health risk', 'too noisy','the neighbours complained', etc.

4. The game continues with fewer and fewer clubs but no-one is knocked out and, as the clubs get more crowded and the dancing more difficult, the need to co-operate increases. The game ends either with everyone in one club or when there is no more room.

Spotlight—Too Babyish

The sad fact is that there is sometimes such a pressure on young people to be cool that they say it's too babyish to play games. The games can be changed to have an older theme. The game Nightclubbing can be recognised as a co-operative version of musical chairs, the under 5s party version. The music should be the sort of music you listen to in nightclubs (try to avoid karaoke!) and, if you don't have music, then it's a chance for communal singing. If it's seen as too babyish, you need to listen and adapt, as it could be the start of a mass walkout from your games session.

Willow in the Wind

Why we like it

It's a trust game with obvious repercussions if you break trust
It can be a very strong experience for the players, particularly the 'Willow'.

How many can do it

7 or more.

Where you can do it

A room where groups of 6 can stand upright in a small circle.

What you might need

Nothing.

Spotlight—Developing Trust

It is easy to spot players who have problems with physical trust games. They:

1. Don't want to join in

2. Have problems letting go or sharing their weight

3. They make it too much of a joke and, in some cases, get very competitive!

4. They sabotage the game by letting people fall or touching inappropriately

Try and spot these players and give them extra support, a chance to opt out, verbal encouragement or clear repeated instructions.

Start your trust games in a calm atmosphere with an introduction about keeping it safe and working together, with everyone taking responsibility. Build up slowly to team games needing more confidence both from you and the players.

If you see a problem, stop the game and try to get the problem sorted. We have a 'stop' rule where, if anyone sees a chance of injury, they can say 'stop' and everyone must stop and check what is needed next.

How you can do it

1. The group forms a circle with 1 member 'the willow' in the centre. Each person in the circle puts their hands on the centre person's shoulders. The person in the centre should stand upright (they can cross their hands over their chest if they wish to) and is instructed to keep their feet together.

2. The 'willow' then lets themself 'fall' in any direction and their weight is taken by the circle who can either pass the willow around the circle or put them back to upright and allow them to fall once more.

3. The aim of the circle is to give the willow a pleasant trust-building experience, not a 'ping-pong ball in a hurricane' experience.

4. If the players are getting rough, you need to calm it down or add extra responsible people to their circle. If the players have managed the hands-on method, then they can catch the central player at greater and greater distances but advise the catching circle to get close in to the faller and to place one foot forward. End the willow's turn and move onto the next volunteer. Volunteering for the task is important as those pressured into the role may find it too threatening.

Safety Check

The group must be able to focus attention and understand their roles and responsibility. The game involves holding the weight of a person briefly so check that there are no physical or health reasons that would mean that a participant should opt out of this game.

Wall Crash

Why we like it

It is a very dramatic trust game

It appears easy

It is a challenge

The group has to keep the individual safe.

How many can do it

Minimum number 6, maximum 30.

Where can you do it

A large empty space with no obstructions. A room must have a diagonal size of 7 m minimum.

What you might need

People to guard immovable obstructions such as pillars, etc.

Snapshot

A group including 3 wheelchair users played this game. Stopping the wheelchair users from getting up speed and crashing into the crowd was a bit of a challenge but resulted in a change of attitude by all the players who realised that the young wheelchair users were a lot less passive than they expected!

How you can do it

1. All the players crowd into a corner of the room with 2 chosen as 'gatekeepers' and one as 'catcher'. The group should attempt, one at a time, to go through the gate and, with their eyes closed, run or walk to get across the diagonal of the room to the opposite corner where the catcher is standing. The idea is to cross the room as fast as possible without opening your eyes. If a runner is going off course or is about to run headlong into the corner for which they are aiming, they need to be slowed down by a gentle grab of the shoulders by the catcher. As soon as one person runs across, she becomes part of the catching team for the next runner.

2. The gateway and gatekeepers are there to ensure that people run one at a time and with a big enough gap between them for runners to be helped by the catching team. As the catching team gets bigger, they can form a funnel of people to slow the next runner. Once they have been caught, the runner should slow down and open his/her eyes.

3. The game can be played with blindfolds but only with a consenting group of young people as the choice of opening your eyes is quicker and less intimidating than taking off a blindfold.

Gateway   Runner   Catchers

Letting Off Steam Games

Spotlight

You may need a few Letting Off Steam games for use when you need something fast and lively—to allow players to express their bounce or to get some bounce back!

Tag games, contact games and running around can be the high-energy part of your session. Even if you are trying to move the group into drama and imaginative play, fast games can get them ready for a bit of reflection and creative thinking. It may be worth interspersing more sitting down activities with letting off steam games.

Amoeba Tag

Why we like it

It has a good ending

It can be very energetic

It is easy to understand.

How many can do it

More than 10.

Where you can do it

Anywhere with space to move about or jump up and down.

Snapshot

We tried Amoeba with a group in an after school club, everyone with their eyes closed. We made sure there were a few people at the edge of the group turning people back towards the middle of the room and the chant of 'amoeba' was started from the person leading the game.

For a less physical ending, all the twos and threes can form into a chain to make a circle.

How you can do it

1. It's a tag game where the tagged players join 1 hand with the person who caught them to form a pair which then catches a third person.

2. When the fourth person is caught, the line of 4 splits into 2 pairs. Both pairs go hunting for more people to join onto their chains. Eventually there are no single players left and, at that point, a chant should be started 'a-moe-ba'. Quiet and slowly at first and then gradually louder as all the pairs or threes join in.

3. At the same time as the chant starts, everyone should try to get to the centre of the room to form one big blobby animal—the amoeba. When people are massed, then they can start jumping up and down, pulsing like one big blob!

4. The end of the game is when people are all bouncing and the leader leads them all into a new game or activity.

Safety Check

When it's jumping, the amoeba can fall and damage smaller participants. The game involves a lot of physical contact so check that players are able to opt out if they want or need to.

Street Child Home

(A street game from Delhi, India)

Why we like it

The game feels very much like a traditional game but it has layers of meaning

You can use it to break the ice for global ideas

The game can break up exclusive groups and get new groups to play together.

How many can do it

15+

Where you can do it

Anywhere you can run about.

Snapshot

This game is a favourite played in the bus station of New Delhi amongst groups of young people who work on the streets. Most of them have no home and many have no family and they use the game to let off steam and to recognise that the game is very central to what is happening in their lives. The 'Butterflies' project uses games, puppets and arts to learn basic skills for survival!

Safety Check

There may be issues to talk about that develop naturally from this game and some may need to be handled sensitively (the words 'child' and 'home' are full of meaning).

How you can do it

1. Everyone gets into threes and each 3 chooses 2 people to make a 'home' by holding both hands and standing facing each other. Tell them that the home has space for 1 child and get the third person to stand in the middle between the arms of the home.

2. Explain the calling system. As caller, you say 'Street child home street child home street child home etc.' Depending on the word you end on, the trio have to respond. If you end with the word 'home', all the 'children' have to stand still whilst the homes move to circle another child. So, without letting go, the 'homes' lift over their first 'child' and find another 'child' to encircle.

3. If you end with the word Child, the 'children' have to get out of the homes and find another home. If you end with the word 'street', all the players get into new threes and choose which pair are going to be home, leaving someone to be a 'child'.

Spotlight

It is possible to have 1 or 2 homeless children if there are not a number that can be divided into threes, which adds more interest, a little competition and the chance to discuss homelessness.

American Football RPS

Why do we like it?

It is lively and involves high energy in bursts

There are moments of quiet and calm, building up to a charge

Being caught does not exclude you but puts you with the 'winners' for the next round

The game is easy to run for young people as long as they are clear of safety elements.

How many can do it

8+

Where you can do it

Indoors or outdoors in a large clear space free from obstructions to running or dangerous sharp objects. 30 m x 10 m is a good sized space (with 5 m for each end zone + 10 m running space from the centre for each team.

Safety Check

The game can easily become full-contact rugby tackling and damaging. Stress the tag nature of 'capturing the opposition'.

How you can do it

1.   Get into 2 roughly equal teams. Set up the space with 2 'touch lines' and 'end zones' and a 'face off' line half way down the room.

2.   The 2 teams are asked to get into group huddles to decide which secret sign they will choose to display at face-off time—they can choose rock paper or scissors—but they must all agree one sign and keep it secret from the other team.

3.   The teams will then face each other in 2 lines. The secret sign is only to be revealed after the caller has counted down from 3 to 1. The whole team should all give the same sign: rock is a clenched fist, paper is a flat hand and scissors is signed by the 2 fingers used in a victory sign.

4.   The rock can blunt the scissors, the scissors can cut the paper and the paper can wrap the rock, and this decides who wins. The team with the winning sign in a face-off should attempt to capture as many of the opposing players as they can by tagging them. The players running away have a 'home' end zone which is safe and if they reach that they can play the next round without having to join the opposing side. In this way, the signs of each team changes each time a round of the game is played.

5.   If both teams show the same sign, then the round is a draw and they go back to huddles to choose their next signs.

6.   The rounds can be played as many times as you like or till one team captures all the opposition players (this may never happen as there is a constant ebb and flow of team members).

Snapshot

We have adapted the game to new themes when we worked in Scotland, for example, with rock, paper, scissors being changed to salmon, midges, wildcat. Wildcats are claws and growls, midges are buzzes and wiggly finger and thumb moves, salmon are hands flapping by your ears like gills and mouth opening and closing like a goldfish. Midges bite cats, cats catch salmon and salmon eat midges.

When we had a group with American children in it, we increased the drama of the event by practising American Football mannerisms such as gum chewing, hunkering down (a sort of gorilla stance) and looking cool, mean and not too clever at the same time.

Spotlight—Playing It Safe

All games can be dangerous if played without being alert or caring! It is important to gently remind players of this. For example, in this American Football game, you can point out how important it is not to impale the opposition on chairs or emboss them on the opposite wall. It is a tag game, not a full contact wrestling match!

Love Handles

Why we like it

There are tactics for avoiding being caught which do not involve fast running

It allows a rapid change of partners

It is possible to play with many people chasing at once.

How many can do it

More than 10.

Where you can do it

A space for running around.

Snapshot

We once played Love Handles as a slow motion game when the area we had to play in was very confined.

In one room, the floor was very slippery and might have been dangerous to run on, so we played in coxed pairs with participants sitting and sliding on their buttocks!

How you can do it

1. Everyone gets paired up with 1 person in front of the other. The person on the rear grasps their partner from behind by the fleshy part of their hips, 'the love handles'. 1 or more are chosen to be those who are hunting for 'lurve'. The others are 'couples', walking around with one in front and the other behind, holding their partner by the rear 'love handles'. The hunters chase the couples and upon catching them, take hold of the love handles on the person at the back. This would make a threesome and therefore an 'unstable' group. The newly grabbed person lets their old partner go and she becomes the new 'lurve hunter'.

2. The game continues until you count how many isolated hunters there are or you just move on to a new game. To speed the game, you can add a rule that couples can split up and both can take on the role of a lurve hunter for a new partner.

Safety Check

It's a physical tag game.

Spotlight

If the title Love Handles is seen as too edgy, then any other paired ideas can be taken on as a way of describing the process, such as, pantomime horses, etc.

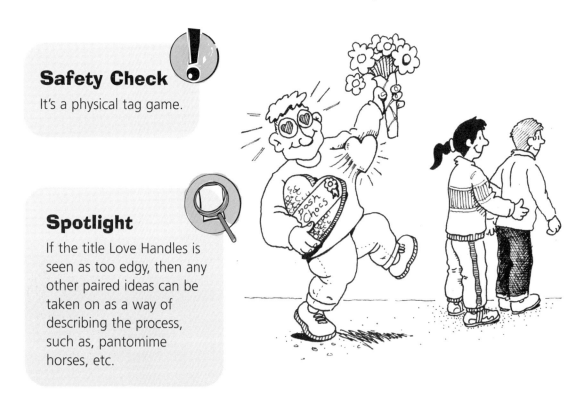

Sticky Toffee

Why we like it

It's a physical game

It promotes teamwork

It allows changing roles.

How many can do it

6 or more.

Where you can do it

A clean and safe floor.

Snapshot

We used Sticky Toffee with a group of very 'physical' young men in a police-sponsored playscheme. They were labelled as 'at risk of offending'. The game allowed them to burn off energy and explore being physical and having fun without injuring each other. It would have been very easy to use the game as a way into a fight but, because we discussed that and gave them support to make safety ground rules, they played the game very fairly and no one ended up in hospital!

How you can do it

Get into threes and decide which one of each group of 3:

1. 'Toffee' whose job it is to stick together in a clump.

2. 'Worker' whose job it is to 'pull the toffee' (remove person sized clumps from the mass).

3. 'Manager' whose job is quality control (that is safety). Make sure that no small bits are pulled and enthuse workers.

Safety Check

This game could potentially become very rough. If the group is not managing safety well, you may need to become a safety supervisor and stop the game to ensure 'quality control'.

Explain all 3 roles clearly. Set all the toffee in an entwined lump on the floor. Check with workers—tickling may be okay, lifting people by the nostrils is not! Managers can enthuse but can also shout 'Stop!' to halt the game.

Once all the toffee is unstuck, that is, in single person chunks, you can swap roles.

Repeat so each person has a chance at each role.

Murder Ball

Why we like it

It's energetic and fun

It's a ball game with no fixed sides

It's good for team-building.

How many can do it

10 or more.

Where you can do it

Largish space, depending on numbers, but big enough for everyone to run around. Clear running around space free of obstacles.

What you might need

Ball, preferably soft.

Safety Check

Watch out for people who can throw balls really hard and make it clear that people can shout 'stop' at any time. Best to use a soft ball and people should only aim below knees.

How you can do it

1. People spread out around the room or space. 1 person is given the ball. Their aim is to tag people by hitting them below their knees with the ball.

2. Once somebody else is tagged, you then have 2 people passing the ball between them to catch more people out.

3. This continues as more and more people are taggers with only a few left trying to avoid the ball. You may have to suggest ways of making it clear who, for example, the taggers holding up their arm to show they are free to catch the ball.

Spotlight—Choosing the First Player

A way of choosing the first person to have the ball (if the group is not too big) is to play Human Pinball. The players stand in a circle, feet apart with no gaps between one player and the next. Players bend down, defending the gap between their legs by clasping their hands together, making a kind of 2-handed fist to push the ball away from the 'goal' between their legs and towards that of another player (it is your job to throw the ball into the middle). Once the ball goes between someone's legs, that person has the ball and Murder Ball can commence. Human Pinball can be prolonged by giving people 3 lives. After 1 life, they must put 1 arm behind their back, after 2 lives, both arms behind, after 3 lives, out.

Snapshot

On a playscheme trip to the beach, we played a team version of Murder Ball called Prisoner. This was an ideal game to play on the beach as it was easy to mark out a rectangular area (pitch) in the sand. We played 4-a-side.

Once the players were on the pitch, we threw the ball into the middle. The aim of each team was to hit opponents below the knees with the ball. Players were allowed to pass the ball between members of their own team. When a player was hit below the knees with the ball, they became a prisoner and had to stand in one area (prison) outside the lines of the pitch. There were 2 'prisons' for members of different teams. This added a new element to the game as their own team could throw the ball over to the 'prison' (trying to avoid interception!) and the prisoners could catch opponents out from behind. Play continued until the whole of one side was caught and imprisoned.

Adapting Sports

Many young people live in dread of sports lessons and sports days, and many adults can recount difficult incidents in competitive sports, for example, picking the team and always being the last one or, worse still, being chosen after the school dog and swapped for a traffic cone! It is worth thinking about ways of picking teams but also about adapting sports to 'even the odds' or to ensure that children with different abilities can be included.

When adapting sports you can think about:

The equipment (bigger, smaller, use 2 balls instead of one?)

The scoring (to promote teamwork)

The pitch (doesn't have to be square—the pitch could be wider at the strongest team's end with a bigger goal)

The rotation (change sides after every goal you score?)

The speed (3-legged versions of games or shuffling on your bottom)

Number playing (larger, smaller, 4 teams, unequal numbers on teams?)

You can do this for 'traditional' playscheme sports such as football and rounders and for unusual ones! You can play golf indoors, play polo using unicycles, row indoors using skateboards and ping-pong bats. You are only limited by your imagination! Try combinations that are inclusive and fun, they may also build skills and promote sharing, trust, communication and teamwork. That would be a way of everyone winning!

Snapshot

This is an example of how we have adapted a game of rounders. There were things that we didn't like about the game: the ball was too hard to hit, the ball was hard to catch, the diamond circuit was huge for the smaller ones, and with a big team you had to wait for ages for your turn.

Although some people say that the rules of the game should be sacred, once we broke that then we could have a bigger ball and bat, such as, a tennis racket. The bowler agreed to give easy and friendly bowls. We even tried placing the ball on top of a traffic cone, like a golf tee, and created different sized diamond circuits marked with hard, medium and easy routes.

Parachute Games

Spotlight

If you have never seen or played with a playchute, be prepared for a fantastically adaptable piece of play equipment almost on a par with a big cardboard box for play value! The parachutes come in a variety of diameters with different size centre holes, some with handles around the edge, some as colourful as rainbows, others as drab as armed forces surplus or from parachute flying clubs. But more and more people use specially made parachutes of ripstop reinforced nylon.

They can be repaired relatively easily if they rip and will last for many years if treated with a tiny bit of care and a lot of enthusiasm.

A 5 m chute is big enough for 20 young people, a 6 m for 30.

Advice about parachutes with handles—cut them off. They are generally restricting to fun and could present health and safety risks as the children may not be able to let go of a handle that has been wrapped around their wrists.

This section includes a range of parachute games, chosen not because they are just favourites but to give a range of different uses of the chute and a taste for the way games can be altered and changed to make them stay fresh. There are some useful starter games to get a group focussed and able to work the parachute together, but we have started parachute sessions from any game and, given the right circumstances, any game can lead to another.

You can buy parachutes from:

Seamstress, 23 Banbury Road, Byfield, Northants, NN11 6XJ
Tel. or fax: 01327 263933
www.playchutes.com

Mushroom

Why we like it

It is a very good starting game for a parachute games session

It is a gentle game

It can be adapted. For example, using words important to the group or any theme that you are doing at the time.

How many can do it

8 or more.

Where you can do it

Wherever you can spread a parachute.

What you might need

Parachute.

Snapshot

For one group we learned the numbers 1, 2, 3 in Japanese and the Bengali word for mushroom. This gave recognition to 2 of the cultures represented amongst the young people and some young people were surprised that their friends could speak other languages!

How you can do it

1. Everyone holds the edge of the parachute. Spread all the players so that they are evenly spaced around the parachute. Ask them to lower the parachute to the ground and stretch it out. Ask everyone to join in a call of 'one, two, three...mushroom'. On the word 'mushroom', you all raise the parachute as high as possible without pulling neighbouring players off their feet. Everyone should then work together to bring the parachute back down.

2. The call (one, two, three and the word to signal the raising of the parachute) can be changed following the suggestions of the players. This can be using different languages to learn numbers or words and using a word that is significant or exciting for the group to get the parachute raised. For example, 'un, deux, trois... boing'! or 'pear, apple, orange... fruit bowl'! The best words will be the ones that come from the group (if they are not too rude!)

Safety Check

If small people are next to larger people, make sure they aren't lifted off the ground or they may dislocate their shoulders.

Walking on Water

Why we like it

The looks of surprise when a 'sunny day' lifts the participant up off the ground!
It's always a popular game—a common problem is having to stop the game before everyone's had a turn!

How many can do it

Enough to give lots of support around the edges of your parachute.

Where you can do it

Space for a parachute. Can be played almost anywhere, but bear in mind that the person on the parachute may land on the ground at some point.

What you might need

Parachute.

Safety Check

Again, remember that the ground must be safe. Warn participants that they shouldn't let go of the parachute suddenly. Warn the person walking on the parachute not to go too close to the hole in the middle.

Snapshot

To make this game more personal, we often pretend that the 'water' is local to our group—even a neighbourhood stream can work.

We've also played this game as a moon environment with participants trying to walk like spacemen around the parachute. 'Rain' can become meteor shower, 'whirlpool' can be a black hole, 'wind' could be blast-off, etc.

How you can do it

1. Players pull the parachute out at waist height. Explain that the parachute is the sea and that you are going to look at how it is affected by different weather.

2. First of all, practice a 'sunny day'. The parachute is pulled as taut as possible by all the participants holding on tight and leaning back. Next, try 'rain', with the players clapping one hand on the top of the parachute. A 'slight breeze' can follow, where the parachute is gently wafted up and down, leading to a gale force wind with lots of furious flapping. You can also try 'a whirlpool' with everyone walking round in a circle or by passing the parachute left person to person. If you're feeling very adventurous, you could change this half way to 'an Australian whirlpool' which basically means turning the parachute the other way. Lastly, you could try 'a tidal wave'—everybody walks forward, holding their bit of the parachute up in front of them.

3. The next step of this game is to pick someone who is brave enough to 'walk on water'. This volunteer must walk around in a circle on top of the parachute—remind them not to get too close to the edges or too close to the hole in the middle. You may want to ask them to take their shoes off before they climb onto the parachute because it's gentler on the parachute material and adds to the slipperiness of the game. As the volunteer walks around, call out different weather forecasts for the other participants to create. Remind them not to suddenly let go because a fairly light person can be lifted quite high on a 'sunny day'.

4. Also, bear in mind that a tidal wave straight from a sunny day could lead to a sudden thud! Once your volunteer falls over, another has a go.

Once the game is established, you can pass on the responsibility of calling out the weather forecasts to others.

Baywatch

Why we like it
It can be noisy and energetic
Everybody gets to join in.

How many can do it
10+

Where you can do it
Enough space for your parachute, with room for a couple of
'lifesavers' to run around the outside.

What you might need
Parachute.

How you can do it

1. Everyone stands around the parachute, holding it at waist height (you can also play this game with players sitting down).

2. Explain that the parachute is going to be the sea and that, lurking within, is a fearsome shark. If you want, you can encourage players to imitate the Jaws soundtrack (der dum, der dum, etc.).

3 Tell them that the shark is going to grab their knees and eat them and that, if they are grabbed, they should scream. Ask them to practice screaming (if they are inhibited, they may need gentle provoking to get going, for example, 'That's it? It must be a very gummy shark. I'm sure if a shark grabbed me I'd scream much louder than that. Let's try again').

4. Choose a volunteer to be the first shark. You also need to choose a couple of 'Baywatch babes or hunks' who are going to run around the outside of the parachute trying to rescue screaming victims. Explain that (unless they are rescued) shark victims go underneath the parachute and become a shark too. Near the end of the game, nearly everyone will be under the parachute.

5. Send your first shark underneath, tell your Baywatch babes and hunks to get ready. Start your 'Jaws' music and make gentle waves with the parachute. It should only be seconds before you hear your first scream.

Snapshot

On a local playscheme, the parachute didn't have to be the sea—the parachute was our local river. Sharks became killer eels, mutant shopping trolleys, etc. Use your imagination - the players did!

Safety Check

Watch out for overly enthusiastic sharks—you don't want somebody dragged underneath so forcefully that their head hits the floor! You can always suggest that sharks tickle knees rather than grab them.

Mexican Wave

Why we like it

It's a good calming game

It encourages teamwork and there is a great sense of achievement when complete circuits are made.

How many can do it

Enough to fit around parachute - not too few or it won't work.

Where you can do it

Anywhere spacious enough for your parachute.

What you might need

Parachute and football (or any other ball).

Snapshot

We played this on a big environmental fun day in a park in Swansea. We played this with a giant Earth ball (a ball with the continents and oceans painted on it). Protecting the planet (or was it themselves?) added even more excitement to the game and the sight of a 2 m ball rolling around on a parachute got people very excited.

How you can do it

1. This game can take some practice. Ask if anyone knows what a 'mexican wave' is. Give examples such as football matches and big sporting occasions like the Olympic Games.

2. Each person must wait until his neighbour has raised and lowered his arms before she takes her turn. You can practice it with just your arms, and then do it whilst holding the parachute.

3. Once you have mastered this, it is time to put the ball onto the parachute. The aim is then to get the ball to make a complete circuit of the parachute without anybody touching it—it may take some practice! To do it successfully, everyone must keep their bit of the parachute low until the ball has gone past them.

4. Once the ball has gone past them, lift and lower.

5. See how many circuits you can do without stopping, and try changing direction. Be prepared for a cheer when it all goes right!

Safety Check

Usual parachute safety rules. Watch out for people running after the escaping ball

Football

Why we like it

It is easy to play

It's an especially good activity for drawing children who like a little competition in their play, but gives everyone an equal chance in an enjoyable, not too energetic, game of football. Having said this, it can be a good way of getting rid of surplus energy

It can be good fun trying to predict results of matches in real football

It leads nicely into Mexican Wave.

How many can do it

16+

Where you can do it

A space large enough for participants to stand easily around a parachute. Not near a road.

What you might need

Parachute or football
(preferably soft).

Snapshot

There was a 5-a-side football competition in the town centre and we were asked to play parachute games to keep the young people busy between matches. We played football with the footballers and used referees' whistles and linesmen's flags to add drama to the game (though we used a large sponge ball printed with football style hexagons not a hard football).

How you can do it

1. Choose 2 football teams of any standard you like. Going around the parachute (held at waist height) alternately label participants for each team, for example, 'Man United' and 'Chelsea'. You may hear a few groans, but, if participants feel very strongly, they could always swap places with their neighbour (some people take their team very seriously!).

2. Make sure the teams are spread evenly by asking every member of one team to put up their hands. If you have 3 in a row, you have some reorganising to do. Team A will have a set time (for example, 2 minutes) to score as many goals as possible.

3. They do this by trying to bounce the ball off the parachute. You will have to decide whether a ball going down the hole in the middle counts as a goal or counts against them as a home goal.

Safety Check

Usual parachute issues. Eager people running after football (under chute, into walls, etc.). Watch out for hard balls versus heads, windows, etc.

4. Team B defend by trying to stop the ball going off the parachute. Make it clear that hand balls and kicking the ball are not allowed. Headers are up to you! Count down the last 10 seconds, then the teams swap over.

Dive for Treasure

Why we like it

It's fun and energetic
It provides an opportunity to perform
There are lots of possible adaptations.

How many can do it

10 or more.

Where you can do it

Somewhere with enough space to spread out a chute.

What you might need

Parachute.

How you can do it

1. Everybody stands round holding the chute at waist height and making waves. Each person removes a shoe and throws it under the chute into a loose pile in the middle.

2. Take it in turns to take a deep breath 'dive' and bring up a shoe—your own would be nice! If you bring up someone else's, 'flap' it across the chute to him or her.

Safety Check

Beware of over enthusiastic monsters.

Snapshot

On one occasion we added a monster to guard the shoes—it held divers until they ran out of air and then they had to stay under the chute like rocks.

We tried a 'blind' octopus to listen for a team of divers.

We also used this game as a way of sorting a group into pairs. Half the group were instructed to throw a shoe under the parachute while the other half were instructed to dive for a shoe and return it to it's owner. They then paired up with the owner.

Animal Shelter

Why we like it

When a parachute is first stretched out it is almost inevitable that players will 'waft' it up and down as fast as they can—this game makes good use of this!

It is so simple and everyone loves playing it.

How many can do it

Enough people for the parachute to be supported around the outside (depends upon the size of the parachute).

Where you can do it

A space large enough to spread out a parachute, with not too low a ceiling!

What you might need

A play chute with a clear hole in the middle (chutes with netting or string across the middle won't work). Also a small pretend animal (for example, a teddy, puppet or soft toy).

Safety Check

Usual parachute health and safety. Also, you may find that when your animal gets 'home', everybody rushes underneath to grab it. You can prevent this by allocating somebody to do the job beforehand.

How you can do it

1.   The parachute is stretched out at waist height.

2.   Show your chosen soft toy or animal and explain that it needs help to find shelter or to get home (this could be for any number of reasons: it got lost in a storm, was chased by a bigger furry animal, etc.). Home, of course, is down the hole in the middle of the chute, and to get the toy down they have to waft the parachute up and down.

3.   This may mean that the parachute is lifted up and down very fast and energetically. If so, suggest going more slowly to see if they have more luck.

Snapshot

During an environmental festival, we had more than one animal on the go and let them race! We split the players into teams around the parachute, each backing 1 animal (making sure teams had members spaced evenly around the parachute by going around and allocating them.

Blob

Why we like it

It's energetic

It develops teamwork

It gathers the group together.

How many can do it

10 or more people.

Where you can do it

Big safe place.

What you might need

Parachute.

Snapshot

One playscheme group enjoyed playing Blob so much that they tried to get their 'blob' to move around over a series of obstacles, chasing over chairs, under tables and through narrow doorways as one big wobbly blob! They even started using a stopwatch to time their assault course.

How you can do it

1. This is a tag game. Fold the parachute in half and put it on a player (the 'catcher') cape-style. The parachute is poisonous and sticky. People should avoid it.

2. The catcher sets off, trailing a cape. As people are tagged they get absorbed into the blob and a larger blob emerges as 2, 3 or 4 people spread the chute out and hunt for others. When numbers caught are sufficient, they can spread the chute out in a circle, holding it with 1 hand and using the other as a 'catching tentacle'. This large and hard to maneuver creature then hunts down the last survivors!

Safety Check

Be careful of children falling and being dragged by the parachute.

Hunter and Hunted

Why we like it

It's energetic and inclusive

It provides an opportunity to perform

It has a rapid turnover of players

It is adaptable

It's one of the most popular games requested by young people whilst playing parachute games.

How many can do it

15 or more (depends on the size of the chute).

Where you can do it

Somewhere with space for a parachute and with a suitable floor for crawling.

What you might need

Parachute.

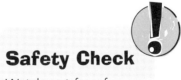

Safety Check

Watch out for of pouncing cats.

How you can do it

1. Stand around the edge of the parachute and hold it at waist height.

2. Set the scene to recreate a cat and mouse chase. Pick a cat and a mouse (it is safer and funnier to pick a cat smaller than the mouse). Common methods here are to pick a cat with a wiggly nose and a mouse with the best teeth or squeak.

3. When the game begins the cat goes on top of the parachute and the mouse underneath, both on all fours. Everyone else is the mouse protection league, making waves, shouting 'over there!', pointing and generally trying to confuse the cat. Remind the cat to catch the mouse, and not leap on it or beat it up!

4. You can add extra mice or cats, or swap tired cats for new ones.

Snapshot

We've played versions of this game using different themes:

'Men in Black' vs space aliens or politicians searching for a policy or 'Jurassic Park' with veloceraptors and humans. As long as there are hunters and hunted, the game works.

During and environmental Fun Day, we played a series of versions as an environmental awareness game—road driver vs hedgehog, fox vs hare, human vs rare animal and talked about these impacts. It also allowed for lots of different actions, noises and movements.

One holiday play scheme used 2 parachutes to make a 3 layered game. The top parachute had a 'dog' on it looking for the cat on the next parachute who was escaping the dog whilst looking for a mouse under that parachute. It was chaotic fun!

Noise Orchestra

Why we like it

It can be good for passing control to different people

It can produce lots of exciting and magnificent noises

Those who are not keen on speaking may make interesting noises

You can introduce all sorts of musical ideas—silence, rhythms, loudness and softness, building up and layering sounds.

How many can do it

12+ (however many fit).

Where you can do it

Under a tent made in a parachute.

What you might need

Parachute. Noise makers can be used.

Safety Check

Be aware of people who may feel claustrophobic under a parachute. If people get particularly hot and bothered under the parachute, you can get half the players to fan the other half by coming out, holding the edge and wafting it up and down together.

How you can do it

1. Everyone gets into a tent made of the parachute, choosing someone as the 'tent pole'. Everyone else should pull the chute down behind their backs and then sit on the outer edge.

2. Under the tent, try to get suggestions for a number of different noises to be the sound of your noise orchestra. Split the people under the chute into smaller groups and allocate each group a noise. The conductor works out a code of signals that mean start, stop, louder, softer, faster, slower, etc. and then starts to play their noise symphony by pointing at certain groups in the orchestra. Be kind to your tent pole or choose someone who's prepared to stick around for a while.

3. Stories or themes can be attached to noises (for example, noises from the body, such as, heartbeats, gurgles, breaths, squidges, chomping and straining, or noises from a haunted house, such as, groans, squeaks of doors, howls of wolves, cries of banshees and clanking chains, or noises from the rainforest, such as, snakes, monkeys, birds and big cats, and the occasional Tarzan!

The games that allow stories and drama can be great starters for helping young people to perform.

Stopping a game while it is still buzzing can often mean that the players will want to play it again another time.

Small Space and Small Groups

Spotlight

You may have a very restricted space for playing games, but it is still possible to use imagination and cunning to make the game fit to the space. Changing tennis to table tennis kept the game fast, skilful and exciting and kept the main spirit of the original for a small spaced indoor game.

Knowing small group games is also a very useful asset, either when there are little groups or as a way of gently persuading more and more players to join in. The enjoyment of a few will spark the interest of spectators to give it a go. The older the group, the more the concept of not wanting to lose their hard earned 'cool' will stop them from joining in. They could be hiding any enthusiasm they may feel for playing together and so, if you can persuade some to join in, you can get them all going.

Moonwalking

Why we like it

It makes people laugh

It is physical and high contact, but only with arms and hands touching

It is possible for a very large person to be boosted by small people.

How many can do it

Groups of 3 (3, 6, 9 etc.).

Where you can do it

Space with a reasonable (2.5 m) ceiling height.

Safety Check

Ensure that people know that it is not their job to lift but to boost everyone to build up to massive leaps!

How you can do it

1. Get everyone into groups of 3 and get the 3 to stand side by side. The players in the middle of the 3s will be the first to moonwalk, and the people on either side of them will be the boosters. The moonwalkers must hold their arms rigidly by their sides to make the 'boost' work. It helps if they ball their hands into fists and their boosters hold onto their fists and elbows. The moonwalker has to work together with the two boosters by:
1. Leaping up and down at regular intervals
2. Keeping their arms straight with locked elbows

2. The boosters time their extra lift so that, each time the moonwalkers jump, they will get a little higher.

3. When this enhanced bouncing is working well, the threesome can try a few more advanced moves, helping the moonwalker to walk weightlessly and in slow motion around the room, trying to avoid other moonwalkers. The 3 can swap roles so everyone tries it!

One Small Step....

4. Some people get the timing of the boost for moonwalking right first time and end up with the middle person bouncing higher and higher and landing lightly between bounces.

5. Other threes do not work well as a team and either hardly get the middle person up in the air at all or end up with the middle person lifting off on a diagonal with one booster working well and the other hardly doing anything. This makes moonwalking a really good team working game which leaves people elated or giggling helplessly.

39 Steps

Why we like it

It gets people paired up

It is great for getting the heart beating a bit faster

It is a good activity to make people smile

A good time filler—5 minutes

A good re-focus game.

How many can do it

Groups of more than 10 to create a silly enough atmosphere.

Where you can do it

Any space where pairs of the group can stand and jump!

Safety Check

The bouncing aspect of this game could give people with bad backs a problem.

Snapshot

On one playscheme, whilst we were waiting for a coach to arrive for an outing, we did not have much running around space and so we played 39 Steps outside the playscheme building to burn off some energy and fill some time before the coach arrived.

In one group who were doing some serious consultation work, young participants were getting very fidgety and 39 Steps was a perfect small energy booster between different parts of the day.

How you can do it

1.   Everyone gets into pairs and the instructions are given one at a time. These are as follows.

2.   Think of a number between 1 and 20, but do not tell your partner yet.

3.   After the caller has said 'one, two, three... carrot' (you can use any word here... but silly ones are better), then both participants should shout their number at each other, then try to add the numbers (they probably did not hear properly due to the shouting).

4.   They should all be asked to repeat the number so that they can hear and then add the 2 numbers together (always easier to get information across if everyone isn't shouting across each other).

5.   The pairs should now stand back to back and link arms.

6.   You should then bounce up and down as many as 40 times, the same number of times as the sum they have just completed... as a pair!

7.   Unless you wish to add any intermediate steps to make the game sillier, more fun or just last longer, that's it.

 ## What next?

The game can lead to many more physical trust building activities.

Arguments

Why we like it

It diffuses tension

It is loud

It's funny

It is a good way of getting people to understand that you can express your anger cleanly without harming anyone or anything

It makes people relaxed enough to enter into a discussion.

How many can do it

2 or more.

Where you can do it

Anywhere.

How you can do it

1. Stand in pairs facing each other, approximately one metre apart. You are going to have an argument and the rules are:

No touching

Each player must only use one word (it can't be a name or swear word)

2. As this sounds odd, we usually demonstrate using the words 'children' and 'no' (2 good words to argue with). Allow the argument to continue for a minute or until everyone seems ready to stop.

Safety Check

Remind participants that this is not a physical contact game. No swear words or names can be used.

Snapshot

We had a group argue using objects in the bathroom as their 2 words! For example, 'soap' and 'towel'—we avoided suggesting 2 words from the kitchen just in case players start to shout 'fork fork fork' a lot!

On another occasion, we were leading a group into a puppetry session and therefore used the puppets as the 'arguers'.

4 Up

Why we like it

It is surprisingly difficult and people laugh when they get it wrong

It is a short game to slot in when other things are getting a bit boring or your group cannot concentrate much longer

It is an easy team game to explain.

How many can do it

More than 7.

Where you can do it

Anywhere.

Spotlight—Adapting Games for Inclusion

4 Up is one game you can easily adapt to include all young people—whatever their specific needs. For example if you or members of the group have mobility difficulties, the group may choose to adapt the game so that you need 4 arms raised at any 1 time.

With a bit of imagination and advice from the experts (those who have a particular need for your adapted games) you can adapt any game and the new game could be a lot more fun than the original! Inclusion makes it better for everyone.

How you can do it

1. The group sit in a circle or a clump where they can all see each other. Tell them that they are now on a planet whose gravity only allows 4 people to stand at any time! The strength of this planet's gravity also means that the people can only stand for a maximum of 5 seconds before they have to sit down again.

2. Atmosphere is really thick so nobody can speak, ask for 4 volunteers to begin the game (you can't pick as you're not on the planet—this may cause lots of discussion!)

3. They are not allowed to discuss tactics to begin with.

4. You may need to give groups a running commentary of the number of people standing at any one time to help them to understand the concept of the game. After a few minutes you can get the group discuss tactics for keeping 4 people up at all times.

Snapshot

You can do it with parts of the body instead of standing up completely.

You can turn it into a music warm-up game by having only 4 people humming or singing at any on time and for only 5 seconds.

You could also do a face-pulling version, which would lose the chance of getting your body moving but gain some 'ice-breaker' silliness!

Mush Mush

Why we like it

People laugh a lot
It is a game from Greenland in the Arctic.
Nobody is in the centre for long.

How many can do it

10–15 people work best.

Where you can do it

Enough space to sit on floor in a circle.

What you might need

Glove, soft shoe or hat.

Spotlight—Turn-Taking Games

In games which involve turn-taking where you don't have time for everyone to take a turn, make sure the players have clear information and can negotiate so that it feels fairer and the players have some degree of control over who gets to have a turn.

How you can do it

1. Participants sit in a tight circle, feet to the centre, knees raised so they form a kind of circular tunnel underneath the knees around the group.

2. The next step is to practice passing a glove, shoe or hat around quickly through the tunnel. A willing volunteer then stands in the middle of the circle and his job is to spot the object. The group has to manoeuvre it round to behind the person then quickly slap them on the bum! This process is helped as the volunteer in the centre often bends forward and turns slowly! Allow time for the glove, shoe or hat to be hidden again. If you are spotted moving the glove, shoe or hat, you go to the centre.

3. If you are hit, you can pick the next spotter. Players can shout 'mush mush' (for reasons which escape us!), bang the floor with their hands and make false passing movement to confuse and divert.

Snapshot

We used a puppet shark for one game of Mush Mush. The shark popped up behind the player to provide a natural attack, like Jaws, the movie. The atmosphere was built up by the players singing the 'der dum, der dum' shark theme to the person in the middle.

Liar

Why we like it

It's fun

It provides a gentle opportunity to take the spotlight

It's creative.

How many can do it

5 or more.

Where you can do it

Somewhere with enough space for people to stand in a circle.

Snapshot

On one occasion, the group started off with fairly everyday suggestions such as making tea or kicking a football, before starting down the road of graphic and medical ideas. 'Having a baby' produced lots of surprises from the boy who did it who showed that he had drama skills and had been watching graphic editions of Casualty!

We have developed this game to use in consultation, for example, mimes about things young people like or don't like doing in their spare time or the best thing they've done in youth club this year, what they'd like to be when they're older, what they're good at (self esteem booster).

How you can do it

1. Explain that this is a game about lying. The group sit or stand in a circle and have 1 person in the middle to begin a mime, for example, digging a garden. A second person should come up and asks 'What are you doing?' and the first person lies 'I'm cleaning an ostrich'.

2. The second person now has to mime this new suggestion and the first person should return to the circle. A third person calls from the circle and asks 'What are you doing?'.

3. The second person gives a new lie, for example, 'combing out my long golden hair' and the third person has to try the new mime and make up a new lie (and so on, in a cycle).

4. Try to encourage and support everyone to come into the middle or at least to whisper suggestions. You can inject some interesting, surreal or strange suggestions which will get people's imaginations going.

Safety Check

Beware of over enthusiastic mimes or rude, offensive suggestions.

End, Celebration and Wind-Down Games

Snapshot

It is useful to signal the end of a games session in some way: to play games that round things off or end on a calm group activity where working together towards a natural conclusion makes everyone feel that they have achieved something as a group.

The end games may lead naturally on to some form of checking how the group feels—what they want to do next and particularly what bits worked for them.

You may need to talk to everyone, plan for the next time you meet or thank people and say goodbye. Whichever you do at the end of your games session, it's nice to have something that feels like a bringing together and celebrating you group's successes.

Prui

Why we like it

It's a game that starts off with a bit of story-telling to explain the rules

It's a trust building game

It's very calm and fairly quiet

It ends up with the whole group holding hands and can therefore lead on to some good whole group circle games.

How many can do it

More than 15 including safety monitors.

Where you can do it

Anywhere with a clear safe walking space.

Safety Check

It's a blindfold game so you need people to patrol the edges and keep the wanderers pointed back towards the middle.

How you can do it

Tell the group that you are now the only creatures on a faraway world. These creatures are gentle and friendly but they have 2 very different stages in their lives.

1. The toddler phase where the creature (called the Prui because of their baby cry!) can make 1 sad and rather hopeful cry, 'prui' (pronounced proo-eee) which they make whenever they touch hands with other Prui. The toddler Prui cannot open their eyes yet and will only become adults by hand-to-hand contact with another adult.

2. The second phase of the creature is the adult phase, the adults can see but they have lost their voices and cannot make a noise. Another feature is that adult Pruis are gluey Pruis so if you grab their hands, you become stuck and part of a growing colony of silent sticky adults!

When the toddler Prui holds hands with another toddler, they both say 'Prui' and that tells them that their hunt for an adult is still going on.

You can tell them to let the other toddler go gently so you don't make them too disappointed!

3. As more and more of the group get stuck to the adults, the plaintive cries of 'prui' get less and less until only one lone toddler Prui is wandering about with their eyes closed in search of an adult hand.

As the game draws to its sticky end, there are a group of players—all holding hands—that can be led (silently as adult Pruis cannot talk) into a circle for a natural chance to thank the group and say 'goodbye'.

Gur Circle

Why we like it

It is a very good group end game

It is quite easy to make it work

It is quite gentle and good for showing physical trust.

How many can do it

8 or more (preferably an even number).

Where you can do it

A large enough space for the whole group to make a circle holding hands with their arms outstretched.

Snapshot

With a group that worked really well together, we did the whole exercise with everyone's eyes closed as a real concentration piece. We then got the circle to lean in and out in time to a slow breathe, so, using someone to count 1, 2, 3, 4 slowly, we were breathing and moving at the same time. The whole group seemed to be moving like one big breathing machine!

How you can do it

1. Everyone holds hands (preferably wrists in a hand to wrist shared grip) in a circle.

2. The group are then divided into 'ins' and 'outs' alternately (in, out, in, out, etc.). An even number in the group means an 'in' will always have two 'outs' and vice versa. You make sure everyone is standing straight and then after a countdown from 3, you say 'Lean!'

3. This signals the 'ins' to slowly lean in and the 'outs' to slowly lean out until their arms are fully extended and their whole bodies are balanced against the counter-weight of their neighbours. This forms a structure a little like the wall of the Mongolian mobile house or 'Gur'.

4. You can then give a countdown to change and the 'ins' will lean out and the 'outs' in.

5. If this is managed smoothly, it looks very impressive.

Safety Check

If played too enthusiastically a player could end up slipping back or falling onto their face so emphasise safety.

Sitting Circle

Why we like it

It is a quite spectacular end game

It does not always work first time

It shows how important everyone's contribution is as one person can bring everyone tumbling down.

How many can do it

Minimum of 8, ideally 12 or more.

Where you can do it

A space flat and clear enough to make a circle of the group shoulder to shoulder.

Safety Check

There could be too much physical contact in this game for some people who need plenty of personal space.

How you can do it

1. Get everyone to stand in as perfect a circle as possible, shoulder-to-shoulder. You can tell the tale of French soldiers in the Napoleonic war retreating from Moscow in the cold, trying to sleep without freezing. Get everyone to point with their right hand towards the centre of the circle and to turn so that their pointing hand is still to the centre but their bodies are now facing sideways.

2. Now get everyone to move or shuffle towards the centre so they are standing as close as possible to the person who is now beside them. This should mean that the circle is still perfect and everyone is now standing ready for the tricky part.

3. Check that everyone is Ok with the next move which will end up with everyone sitting on someone's lap and having someone sat on their lap.

4. Ask everyone to reach forward and hold onto the hips of the person in front of them.

5. Check for any big gaps in the circle and help people to shuffle in to fill them.

6. You can get everyone to practice 2 things to say: one is 'stop'. Anyone saying this has to be obeyed by the whole group to keep it safe. The other phrase is 'sit on my knees please!' Tell people that, as long as they keep their legs together to make a good lap and help the person in front of them to lower themselves onto their laps, they will all be able to sit down in one big sitting circle.

7. The word 'please' is the keyword. Tell them not to lower the person in front of them down into their laps until they have said 'please'. When the circle is seated, see if you can hold it steady.

8. You can let go of hips and wave your hands in the air. If the circle is really stable, you should be able to shuffle forward right leg, left leg, right leg (this may result in a wave of bottoms hitting the floor!).

Acknowledgements for
Games for 10–14 year olds

Thousands of young people, including our own children, whose ideas have been absorbed, explored and adapted in playing with us.

Ali John and Associates for getting our heads around issues of inclusion playfully.

Seamstress for providing almost indestructible and beautiful parachutes and for sharing ideas for new games.

Claire O'Kane and the Butterflies Project in Delhi, India, for their street work ideas

Dave Potter and the Greenaway family, Playright, Interplay, Play Wales, Parasol and the Albion Kids Show, Hackney for giving us space and inspiration to be playful.

All other authors of co-operative and creative play books, particularly

> Terry Orlick for *Cooperative Sports and Games*, Books 1 & 2, published by Writers and Readers Publishing Cooperative, London.

> Donna Brandes for *The Gamesters Handbook*, published by Stanley Thornes, 1998. ISBN 0748735046

> Dave Ruse for *City Adventures,* published by Paul Chapman, London, 1989.

> Mildred Masheder for *Let's Play Together*, published by Green Print, London, 1989. ISBN 1854250094.

It is hard to determine the real origins of games, so we apologise if we haven't credited you and you think we have stolen your ideas!

Dedicated to Otto Bassel and to Olaf Burton, my guide and mentor.